EARLY PEOPLES

THE AZTEC

WORLD
BOOK

World Book
a Scott Fetzer company
Chicago
www.worldbookonline.com

World Book, Inc.
233 N. Michigan Avenue
Chicago, IL 60601
U.S.A.

For information about other World Book publications, visit
our Web site at **http://www.worldbookonline.com** or call
1-800-WORLDBK (967-5325).
For information about sales to schools and libraries, call
1-800-975-3250 (United States), or **1-800-837-5365 (Canada)**.

Library of Congress Cataloging-in-Publication Data

The Aztec.
    p. cm. -- (Early peoples)
    Includes bibliographical references and index.
    Summary: "A discussion of the early Aztec, including who
the people were, where they lived, the rise of civilization, social
structure, religion, art and architecture, science and technology,
daily life, entertainment and sports, and fall of civilization.
Features include timelines, fact boxes, glossary, list of recommended reading and web sites, and index"--Provided by
publisher.
    ISBN 978-0-7166-2133-1
    1. Aztecs--Juvenile literature. I. World Book, Inc.
F1219.73.A94 2009
972'.01--dc22
                                                    2008020110

Printed in China
1 2 3 4 5 13 12 11 10 09

STAFF

EXECUTIVE COMMITTEE
President
  Paul A. Gazzolo
Vice President and Chief Marketing
Officer
  Patricia Ginnis
Vice President and Chief Financial Officer
  Donald D. Keller
Vice President and Editor in Chief
  Paul A. Kobasa
Director, Human Resources
  Bev Ecker
Chief Technology Officer
  Tim Hardy
Managing Director, International
  Benjamin Hinton

EDITORIAL
Editor in Chief
  Paul A. Kobasa
Associate Director, Supplementary
Publications
  Scott Thomas
Managing Editor, Supplementary
Publications
  Barbara A. Mayes
Senior Editor, Supplementary Publications
  Kristina Vaicikonis
Manager, Research, Supplementary
Publications
  Cheryl Graham

Manager, Contracts & Compliance
(Rights & Permissions)
  Loranne K. Shields
Administrative Assistant
  Ethel Matthews
Editors
  Nicholas Kilzer
  Scott Richardson
  Christine Sullivan

GRAPHICS AND DESIGN
Associate Director
  Sandra M. Dyrlund
Manager,
  Tom Evans
Coordinator, Design Development and
Production
  Brenda B. Tropinski

EDITORIAL ADMINISTRATION
Director, Systems and Projects
  Tony Tills
Senior Manager, Publishing Operations
  Timothy Falk

PRODUCTION
Director, Manufacturing and Pre-Press
  Carma Fazio
Manufacturing Manager
  Steve Hueppchen
Production/Technology Manager
  Anne Fritzinger

Production Specialist
  Curley Hunter
Proofreader
  Emilie Schrage

MARKETING
Chief Marketing Officer
  Patricia Ginnis
Associate Director, School and Library
Marketing
  Jennifer Parello

Produced for World Book by
  White-Thomson Publishing Ltd.
  +44 (0)845 362 8240
  www.wtpub.co.uk
Steve White-Thomson, President

Writer: Andrew Langley
Editor: Kelly Davis
Designer: Simon Borrough
Photo Researcher: Amy Sparks
Map Artist: Stefan Chabluk
Illustrator: Adam Hook (p. 19)
Fact Checker: Charlene Rimsa
Proofreader: Catherine Gardner

Consultant:
Michael E. Smith
Professor of Anthropology
Arizona State University, Tempe, Arizona

TABLE OF CONTENTS

WHO WERE THE AZTEC?	4-5	THE AZTEC CALENDAR	34-35
ORIGINS OF THE AZTEC	6-7	THE GREAT CITY OF TENOCHTITLAN	36-37
BUILDING AN EMPIRE	8-9	LANGUAGE AND WRITING	38-39
THE AZTEC EMPIRE AT ITS HEIGHT	10-11	AZTEC ART AND CRAFTS	40-41
THE TLATOANI AND HIS ADVISERS	12-13	FAMILY LIFE	42-43
COMMONERS AND CALPOLLI	14-15	SHELTER AND CLOTHING	44-45
SOLDIERS AND WARFARE	16-17	FOOD AND DRINK	46-47
MERCHANTS	18-19	CHILDREN AND EDUCATION	48-49
FARMERS	20-21	SPORTS AND FESTIVALS	50-51
AZTEC WOMEN	22-23	TRADE AND TRANSPORTATION	52-53
SLAVES	24-25	DECLINE AND DANGER	54-55
CRIME AND PUNISHMENT	26-27	THE FALL OF THE AZTEC EMPIRE	56-57
BELIEFS AND GODS	28-29	THE AZTEC LEGACY	58-59
CEREMONIES AND HUMAN SACRIFICE	30-31	GLOSSARY	60-61
TEMPLES AND PRIESTS	32-33	ADDITIONAL RESOURCES	62
		INDEX	63-64

Glossary There is a glossary on pages 60-61. Terms defined in the glossary are in type **that looks like this** on their first appearance on any spread (two facing pages).

Additional Resources Books for further reading and recommended Web sites are listed on page 62. Because of the nature of the Internet, some Web site addresses may have changed since publication. The publisher has no responsibility for any such changes or for the content of cited sources.

WHO WERE THE AZTEC?

The Aztec were an American Indian people who lived in **Mesoamerica** (*MEHS oh uh MEHR uh kuh*) more than 500 years ago. They were fierce warriors and great builders. They believed in many gods, and religion ruled nearly all parts of their lives.

The Aztec conquered a great empire in the country we now call Mexico. They ruled large parts of southern and central Mexico in the 1400's and early 1500's. They also built a city that, for its time, was one of the largest in the world. Spanish invaders conquered and destroyed the Aztec empire in 1521.

Where Did the Aztec Live?

The Aztec lived in an area centered on the Valley of Mexico, which is a huge, oval region surrounded by mountains and volcanoes. The climate in this region is warm and mild, and the rich soil is good for growing crops. In the middle of the valley was a large system of lakes. This valley is the site of present-day Mexico City.

▼ The **Pyramid** of the Sun rises 246 feet (75 meters) above the ancient city of Teotihuacan *(tay oh tee wah KAHN)*, near present-day Mexico City. The city was an important religious center for the Aztec, though it was built in about A.D. 100, centuries before the rise of the Aztec. The Aztec believed that the city had been built by an ancient race of giants. Aztec **myths** related that the gods met there and created the world in which the Aztec lived.

▶ A massive sculpture of a head, on display at the Museum of Anthropology *(AN thruh POL uh jee)* in Jalapa *(huh LAH puh)*, Mexico. The head was carved by the Olmec, who built the first major civilization in the Americas along the Gulf Coast in present-day Mexico. They left behind a number of these huge carved stone heads, which **archaeologists** believe were created around 1200 to 1000 B.C.

TIMELINE
BEFORE THE AZTEC

Olmec—from around 1200 to 400 B.C.
The Olmec *(OHL mehk)* built what was probably the first major **civilization** in the Americas. They lived on the Gulf Coast of present-day Mexico. The most famous remains of Olmec culture are giant carved stone heads.

Maya—from around A.D. 250 to 900
During the height of their culture, the Maya *(MAH yuh)* lived in the area where modern Mexico joins Guatemala. The Maya built wonderful buildings and created beautiful paintings and pottery. They also developed their own systems of astronomy, mathematics, and writing.

Toltec—from around A.D. 900 to 1200
The Toltec *(TOHL tehk)* ruled an empire in central Mexico. They founded the first great cities in the region. The Toltec were the most powerful people in what is now the Mexican highlands when the Aztec arrived.

The center of the Aztec empire was the city of Tenochtitlan *(tay nohch TEE tlahn)*. The Aztec built this city on an island in Lake Texcoco *(taysh KOH koh)* in the mid-1300's. The city grew very large and had many magnificent palaces and temples.

The Aztec and the Gods

Religion was very important in Aztec life. People spent much of their time worshiping the gods, either at their home or in a temple. The Aztec people believed that the gods needed fresh blood to keep them strong. Many Aztec religious ceremonies included the killing of prisoners and other victims. Often, these ceremonies took place in temples at the top of pyramids.

ORIGINS OF THE AZTEC

We do not know much about the Aztec before they came to the region that is now central Mexico. They did not keep written records at that time, but they did pass along stories to one another. Much of what we know comes from those stories, which form a mix of oral (spoken) history and **legends.**

According to legend, the Aztec came from a place called Aztlan *(ahs TLAHN),* which means "place of whiteness" or "place of the herons." No one knows for sure where Aztlan was. It might have been in present-day northern Mexico, or it might have been much farther north.

Finding a Home

From the oral history of the Aztec, scholars know that they wandered for many years in search of a new home. They came to the Valley of Mexico in the 1200's. However, other Indian peoples had already settled there, and most of the good land for farming was already taken.

WHAT'S IN A NAME?

Today, the word *Aztec* refers to the American Indians in central Mexico who have similar languages and beliefs. But the people who came from Aztlan did not call themselves Aztec. They were known as the *Mexica (Meh SHEE kuh).* *Aztec* came from the name *Aztlan.* The word *Mexico* came from *Mexica.*

▼ A map of **Mesoamerica** in the early 1500's. The darker area shows the Aztec empire at its height.

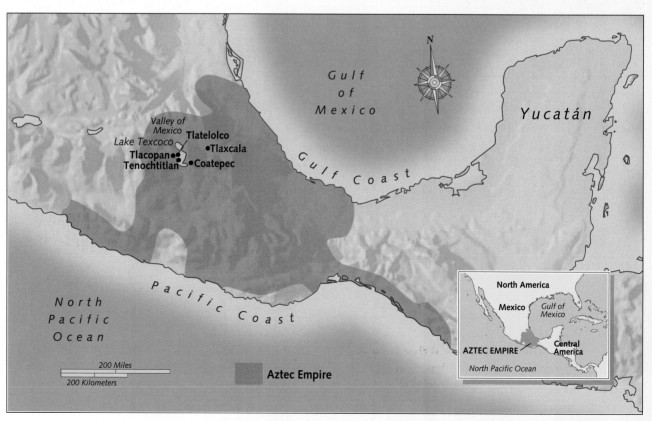

◀ A book cover from the mid-1500's depicts the founding of Tenochtitlan. In Aztec legend, when the first settlers came to Lake Texcoco they found an eagle perched on a cactus on an island in the lake. The Aztec believed this was a sign from the gods to found their city on that island.

The Aztec had a hard time finding a place to live. They settled in a region with few people, but with many snakes. Once settled, the Aztec angered the local king, who sent his army to chase them away. The Aztec found a hiding place in the swamps and shallow waters of the lakes.

The Eagle and the Cactus

In about 1325, the Aztec came to a small island in Lake Texcoco *(taysh KOH koh)*. There, according to legend, they saw an eagle with a snake in its mouth. The eagle was sitting on a cactus, and the Aztec believed this was a sign from one of their gods. They decided to build their new home there.

It may have seemed like a poor place to settle, but there were plenty of fish, birds, and water plants to eat on the island. The Aztec also built up mud fields, called **chinampas** *(chee NAHM pahs)* in the lake, where they grew more food. Most important of all, the water surrounding them was a natural defense against enemies. The Aztec founded the city of Tenochtitlan *(tay nohch TEE tlahn)* on that swampy island.

BUILDING AN EMPIRE

The Aztec had found a home on that small island in Lake Texcoco *(taysh KOH koh)*, but they were still weak, and there were many other groups struggling for power in the Valley of Mexico. During the mid-1300's, the Aztec formed an **alliance** *(uh LY uhns)* with the Tepanec *(tay PAH nayk)* Indians who lived to the west. Aztec soldiers fought for the Tepanec armies in local wars. In return, the Tepanec protected the Aztec from enemies.

The Aztec grew stronger and built a second city, called Tlatelolco *(TLAH tay LOHL koh)*, on the lake. In 1372, they chose Acamapichtli *(AH kahm ah PEETCH tlee)* as their first ruler. The Aztec ruler was known as the **tlatoani** *(TLAH toh AH nee)*. The city of Tenochtitlan *(tay nohch TEE tlahn)* began to expand, as more people came to live there.

TIMELINE OF THE AZTEC EMPIRE

1325 Aztec found the city of Tenochtitlan

1358 They found another city to the north, called Tlatelolco

1372 They elect the first tlatoani, or ruler, Acamapichtli

1428 Aztec form the Triple Alliance with Texcoco and Tlacopan

1440 Montezuma I becomes the fifth tlatoani

1450-1455 Drought kills thousands in the Valley of Mexico

1469 Montezuma I dies

◄The **pyramid** at Tenayuca *(teh nuh YOO kuh)*, just outside present-day Mexico City, was built in stages between the 1200's and the 1500's. Featuring a double staircase typical of Aztec temple design, the pyramid is believed to be similar to, though much smaller than, the Templo Mayor pyramid at Tenoch-titlan (present-day Mexico City), which was destroyed by the Spanish when they invaded in 1519.

The Triple Alliance

By the 1420's, the Tepanec leaders became alarmed by the growing power of the Aztec, and war broke out between the two peoples. In 1428, the Aztec formed a new alliance with two nearby cities, Texcoco and Tlacopan *(tlah KOH pahn)*. This Triple Alliance defeated the Tepanec and destroyed their city.

Soon after this, the armies of the Alliance gained control over the whole Valley of Mexico. Some of the conquered peoples were put to work in Tenochtitlan. One of their first tasks was to build a huge **causeway** that linked the city to the shore of the lake.

The First Montezuma

In 1440, Montezuma I *(MON tuh ZOO muh)* became the fifth tlatoani of Tenochtitlan. Montezuma's name is also spelled Moctezuma *(MOK tay SOO mah)* or Motecuhzoma *(maw TAY kwah SOH mah)*. He strengthened Aztec rule and began building a massive new temple in Tenochtitlan. However, disaster struck the region in the 1450's when a long **drought** caused the crops to fail. Many thousands of the Aztec starved to death in the resulting **famine**.

When the drought ended in 1455, Montezuma was determined that his people should not starve again. He set out to conquer lands to the south and east, where there was plenty of rain and crops grew well. The Aztec army marched over 500 miles (800 kilometers) to invade the empire of the Mixtec *(MEESH tehk)* near the Pacific Coast.

▶ An eagle warrior in a beaked helmet is depicted in a stone carving dating from around 1500. Eagle warriors were the elite troops in the Aztec army and wore special feathered costumes into battle.

The Aztec Empire at its Height

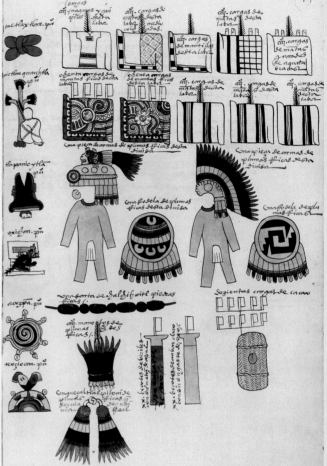

Montezuma I died in 1469. He had extended the Aztec empire to reach the Pacific Coast to the south and the Gulf of Mexico to the north and east. The conquered peoples from the new lands were ordered to send **tribute** to Tenochtitlan *(tay nohch TEE tlahn)*. The tribute included cotton, precious feathers, gold dust, perfumes, and live eagles.

The **tlatoani** *(TLAH toh AH nee)* who ruled after Montezuma I faced several civil wars. The nearest took place in Tlatelolco *(TLAH tay LOHL koh)*, the twin city of Tenochtitlan. In 1473, there was a dispute between the two cities, and the army of Tenochtitlan quickly stormed into Tlatelolco and killed its ruler.

The First Defeat

By the late 1470's, the Aztec empire was one of the most powerful in **Mesoamerica,** but it was not the strongest. In about 1478, the Aztec invaded the land to the west. They came up against the Tarascan *(tuh RAS kuhn)* Indians, who ruled much of what is present-day western Mexico. The Tarascan crushed the smaller Aztec army and forced it to retreat. According to **legend**, only 200 men (out of 24,000) returned to Tenochtitlan. It was the first big defeat for the Aztec. They never attacked the Tarascan again.

Strengthening the Empire

The Aztec empire reached its height during the reign of Ahuitzotl *(ah WIT zot tel)*. He became tlatoani in 1486 and immediately set out to conquer new lands to the north. His armies

▲ The tribute sent to an Aztec emperor from an area he had conquered is illustrated in the *Codex Mendoza (mehn DOH zah)*. This **codex,** or book, was created by Aztec and Spanish authors after the fall of the Aztec empire. Tribute included feathered headdresses, decorated shields, and woven cloaks.

MONTEZUMA II

Born in about 1480, Montezuma II, the great-grandson of Montezuma I, became ruler of the Aztec in 1502. He extended the Aztec empire still farther and built great temples and public works. Despite these accomplishments, many people did not like him. He demanded very heavy taxes from his people, and he gave important jobs to his favorites.

brought back thousands of prisoners, whom the Aztec sacrificed to celebrate the opening of the huge, newly built Great Temple, or Templo Mayor *(TEHM ploh mah YAWR)*, in Tenochtitlan.

Ahuitzotl made the borders of the Aztec empire stronger. He seized control of land to the north and west to protect his territory from the Tarascan. He also invaded areas to the south and east, as far as present-day Guatemala. Ahuitzotl died in 1502. He was succeeded by Montezuma II, the last of the great Aztec tlatoani.

In 2007, Mexican **archaeologists** announced that they had discovered what is thought to be the tomb of Ahuitzotl in Mexico City.

▲ A jaguar's head, carved from stone. The Aztec revered the jaguar as a symbol of strength. At his coronation *(KAWR uh NAY shuhn)*, a new tlatoani sat on a throne padded with jaguar skins. He also cut himself with a sharp jaguar bone to make a sacrifice of blood.

The Tlatoani and His Advisers

A council of **noblemen** chose the **tlatoani** *(TLAH toh AN nee)* from among the men of the royal family. Once chosen, he ruled all the land and people inside the Aztec empire.

The tlatoani was also the religious leader, and he played a major part in religious ceremonies. He was the military leader, organizing wars and even commanding his soldiers in battle. He was also called the "father and mother" of the people. This meant he was responsible for protecting them from **famine** or invasion and making sure they were treated fairly.

The Snake Woman and the Council

The tlatoani had a deputy who ruled the country when the ruler was absent. The deputy was called the "Snake Woman," even though the person who held this position was a man. The position was named for an Aztec goddess, the Earth Mother Cihuacoatl *(SEE wah koh AHT uhl)*, the goddess of birth and of women who died in childbirth. The man who had the position of "Snake Woman" controlled the law courts and the wealth of the royal palace.

Before making important decisions, the tlatoani got advice from his council. The four members of the council were always nobles and were usually senior army leaders. When a tlatoani died, the same council chose someone to replace him.

◀ A shield pendant, dating from around 1500, is thought to symbolize war and bear the sign of a tlatoani of the Aztec empire. Fashioned in gold by Mixtec *(MEESH tehk)* craftsmen, such jewelry was highly prized by Aztec nobles. The piece was found in a Spanish shipwreck near Veracruz.

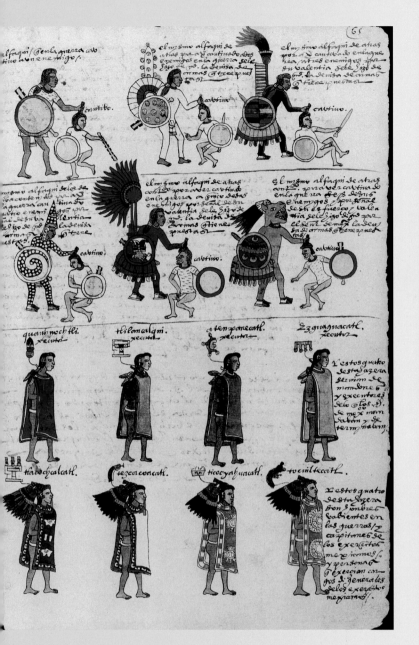

▲ A page from the *Codex Mendoza* shows the six stages in the training of a warrior-priest (top two lines). All the priests are seen holding a prisoner by the hair. Officers of the tlatoani are illustrated in the bottom two lines of this **codex** page.

"MY GREAT LORD!"
Spanish soldier Bernal Díaz del Castillo *(behr NAHL DEE ahth dehl kahs TEEL yoh)* served under Hernán Cortés *(ehr NAHN kawr TEHZ)* and saw the fall of the Aztec empire. His accounts were published in 1632. The English translation of his work, *The Conquest of New Spain*, was first published in 1800. Díaz gives only the Spanish view of events, not the view of the Aztec. Still, Díaz's book is an eyewitness account of his time among the Aztec. Of the tlatoani, Diaz wrote:

"[The emperor] had a guard of two hundred chieftains lodged in rooms beside his own, only some of whom were permitted to speak to him… They had to be clean and walk barefoot, with their eyes downcast, for they were not allowed to look him in the face, and as they approached they had to make three obeisances [deep bows], saying as they did so, 'Lord, my Lord, my great Lord!'"

The Aztec Nobles

With the exception of the tlatoani, the highest rank of people in Aztec society were the nobles. They held most of the powerful positions in government; they made up most of the priesthood; and they controlled nearly all of the empire's wealth.

Nobles also had special rights that set them apart from the rest of the people. They could wear fine jewelry and clothing made of cotton. Nobles were allowed to build houses of two stories. Men who were of the noble class could have more than one wife. Children of this class were educated in special religious schools.

COMMONERS AND CALPOLLI

Most Aztec were commoners and belonged to the class below the **nobles**. The commoner class contained workers of all kinds, including fishermen, craftsmen, farmers, and merchants. Commoners had to pay taxes each year to the **tlatoani** (*TLAH toh AN nee*) or to their local lord. The men also had to serve in the Aztec army during wartime.

The Calpolli

Most commoners lived in groups of families called **calpolli** (*kahl POHL lee*). These groups lived near each other and shared a piece of land. There might be 20 houses in a small calpolli, though some were much bigger. In the countryside, the families of a calpolli would farm their land together. In the towns, the calpolli were the most basic form of government. Each had a council. They might form groups of craftsmen or merchants. The families could pass on their plots of land to their children.

Each calpolli elected its own leader. The families sent their children to the local school, shopped in the local market, and worshiped in the local temple.

Not every commoner belonged to a calpolli. Some poorer people had no land on which to grow crops or build a house. All of their work went to their local lord.

▲ A small stone carving, on display at the National Museum of Anthropology in Mexico City, depicts a free Aztec farmer. Made for a sacrificial altar, the statue shows that farmers of this class wore loincloths made from the fibers of the **maguey** plant. They were forbidden to wear sandals.

◀ Aztec craftsmen use the feathers of tropical birds to fashion headdresses for nobles in an illustration from the *Florentine Codex*. This **codex** was compiled by a Franciscan missionary in about 1570.

Rising to the Top

Commoners very rarely became nobles, but they could rise to more powerful positions in their own **social class.** One way of doing this was by showing great bravery in battle. A soldier who captured a large number of enemy prisoners might gain a higher rank, and he would then be allowed to wear colorful clothing and jewels.

Merchants and craftsmen could also rise to the top of their class by becoming rich or becoming well known for their skills. They might then send their sons to a religious school to train to become a priest. If a son did well there, he could become a high priest. This was a very important position in Aztec society.

SOLDIERS AND WARFARE

Warfare was a vital part of Aztec life. They fought wars for two main reasons. One reason was to defeat other states and force them to hand over their wealth. The second—and most important reason—was religion. The Aztec needed a steady supply of prisoners to sacrifice to their gods.

The main aim of the Aztec when in battle was not to conquer for land, but to capture enemy soldiers and citizens. The Aztec army would spread out in a long line across the battlefield. The soldiers would mock the other side, daring them to charge. Then the two ends of the Aztec line would move forward and try to surround the enemy army.

A Soldier's Training

Nearly all Aztec males had to serve for a time in the army. Boys started their military training at school. Up to the age of 10, boys had their head shaved. Once they began their training, they grew a lock of hair on the back of their head. They were not

▼ A life-sized terra-cotta (baked clay) figure, on display in the Templo Mayor Museum in Mexico City, shows the beak, feathers, and talons worn by the Aztec army's elite eagle warrior class.

EAGLE WARRIORS

The most elite soldiers in the Aztec army—the eagle warriors—were **nobles**. They wore a special costume into battle sewn with real eagle feathers. Their armor included a beaked helmet, armguards in the shape of feathers, and talons (claws) on their knees. The main job of the eagle warrior was to capture enemy prisoners and take them to the temple for sacrifice.

allowed to cut off this lock of hair until they had captured a prisoner in battle.

At school, boys learned how to use weapons and took part in mock battles. Their teachers were usually older soldiers. Then the boys were sent to a real war. At first, they carried equipment for other soldiers. Once they had gained experience, they were allowed to fight.

Weapons of War

Aztec soldiers wanted to capture their enemies alive, so their weapons were designed to wound people rather than kill them. Their main weapon was a **macuahuitl** *(mah kwah WHEET uhl)*, a club made of wood, with pieces of hard, naturally formed glass called **obsidian** *(ob SIHD ee uhn)* fixed to the edge. They also used bows and arrows and spears, all with obsidian points. Obsidian is formed naturally by the heat of volcanoes. (An obsidian blade can be sharper than a modern surgeon's knife.) A special spear-throwing device called an **atlatl** *(aht LAHT uhl)* allowed them to throw their spears over long distances.

◀An Aztec atlatl allowed soldiers to throw their spears over long distances. This example is made of wood covered in gold leaf (thin sheets of gold).

MERCHANTS

Trade was important to the Aztec empire. Merchants, called **pochteca** *(potch TEH ka)*, brought in vital goods and raw materials from other states and from distant countries. They also sold Aztec goods abroad, even as far north as what is now the southwestern United States.

Many pochteca became very rich through their work. They did not belong to the **noble** class but were at the top of the commoner class. This sometimes made life difficult for them. As commoners, merchants were not allowed to show off their wealth. They therefore tried to look poor. They usually returned from their expeditions at night and hid their goods so that no one would see how successful they had been.

A Trading Expedition

The life of a merchant could be dangerous. An expedition might last several months and cover a huge distance. Merchants often traveled in a caravan *(KAR uh van)*, a group of people traveling together for safety. Sometimes robbers or enemy soldiers might attack a caravan. The Aztec had no horses, so the caravan traveled on foot. A team of porters carried goods on their backs.

The merchants went from town to town, visiting markets and buying or selling goods. They could cross borders, even between states at war. For this reason, they often acted as spies for the **tlatoani** *(TLAH toh AN nee)*. He paid them to bring back information about a possible enemy, such as the size of their army.

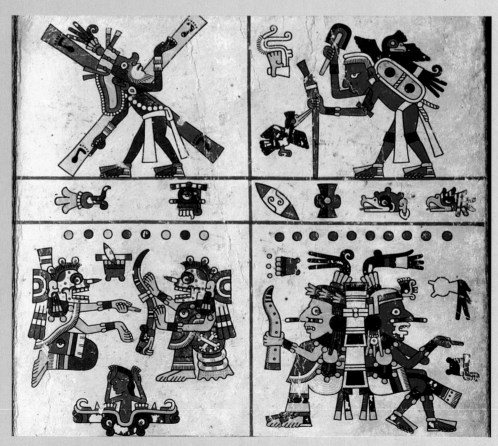

◀The *Codex Fejervary-Mayer (FEH yahr vah ry MAY ehr)*, which dates to sometime before 1521, shows a mixture of images and symbols. The Aztec god of merchants (top left) is shown carrying a crossroads symbol with merchants' footprints coming and going. A merchant (top right) carries a fan and staff and, on his back, a cargo of quetzal *(keht SAHL)* birds.

Markets and Money

Every city in the Valley of Mexico had a marketplace where a huge variety of goods were for sale. Merchants, farmers, craftsmen, and housewives all went there to buy or sell items. Even nobles sent servants to buy food in the markets.

The Aztec had no coins, but they used cacao beans or rolls of cotton cloth as forms of money. Some people also bought things by bartering—exchanging one kind of good for another.

▼ An artist's depiction of an Aztec market.

A Market in Tlatelolco

Hernán Cortés, the Spanish explorer who conquered the Aztec in 1521, described an Aztec market in Tlatelolco *(TLAH tay LOHL koh),* in a letter he sent to Spain:

"There is one square where more than 60,000 people come each day to buy and sell, and where every kind of merchandise is found: provisions [food] as well as gold and silver, lead, brass, copper, tin, shells, bones and feathers. There is a street where they sell game and birds of every species: chickens, partridges and quails, wild ducks, pigeons, parrots, eagles, falcons, sparrow hawks and kestrels. There are streets of herbalists, where all medicinal herbs and roots are sold…"

FARMERS

At least 1 million people lived in the Valley of Mexico in the early 1500's. All of them needed regular supplies of food, so growing crops was a vital task.

Most Aztec farmers had only small plots of land. They used different farming methods in different areas. On the steep slopes of the mountains, the soil was easily washed away by rain. On these slopes, the farmers built **terraces** (*TEHR ihs ehz*), small stone walls to keep the soil in place. In the lowlands, there was not enough rain for plants to grow, so farmers dug long ditches to bring water from the rivers.

▼ The *Florentine Codex,* made by both Aztec and Spanish authors in the mid-1500's, shows an Aztec farmer using a long digging stick with a blade at the end. The Aztec used this tool to plant and cultivate their garden plots.

Crops from the Chinampas

The Aztec even grew crops on the shallow lakes and swamps. To do this, they created artificial islands called **chinampas** (*chee NAHM pahs*). First they scraped up mud from the lake bottom and piled it into mounds mixed with reeds. Then they drove in wooden posts or planted willow trees to hold the edges of the island.

With water readily available, the chinampas produced large amounts of vegetables, fruits, and flowers. They could improve the soil by adding more lake mud, which was very **fertile**. Or they fertilized the soil with water plants that were rich in nitrogen (*NY truh juhn*)—a chemical that most plants need to grow.

Working the Land

Aztec farmers had no plows or carts, and they used very simple tools. They did most of their work with a long digging stick, which had a blade at the end. With this tool, they dug in the soil and scraped over the soil to clear weeds.

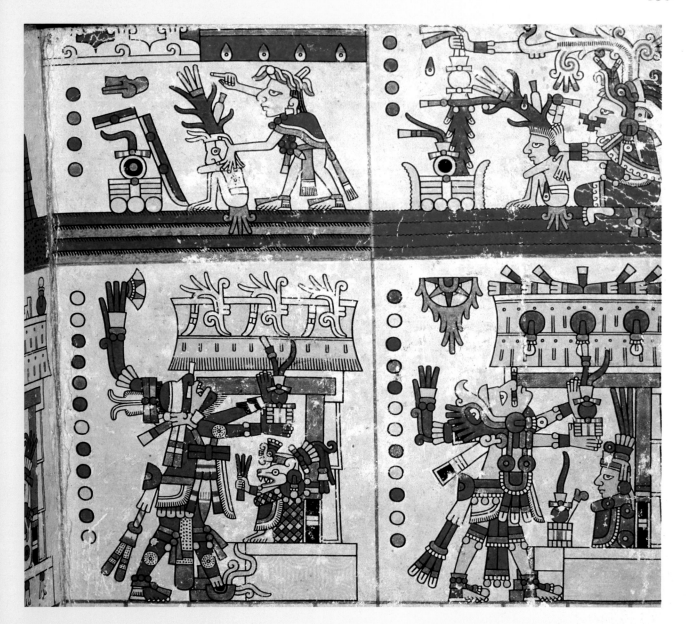

▲ The *Codex Fejervary-Mayer*, painted on deerskin before the 1521 conquest, illustrates the effects of weather on the Aztec's corn crop over a two-year period. In the first year (top right), a goddess pours rain down over a healthy plant. In the second year (top left), the plant withers during a **drought**. The Aztec believed that a single god, Tlaloc *(TLAH lohk)*, was responsible for both plentiful rain and drought.

Beans, corn, squash, sweet potatoes, and tomatoes were the main crops grown by the Aztec. On the drier lowlands, farmers grew cotton, cactus, and **maguey** *(MAG way* or *mah GAY)*, a term for certain types of agave *(uh GAH vee)* plants. Maguey was a very useful plant. The Aztec made cloth from the leaves, sewing needles from the sharp spines, and medicines and an alcoholic drink from the juice.

WHERE WERE THE ANIMALS?

During the time that the Aztec ruled, there were no horses, cattle, hogs, or sheep in the Western Hemisphere. They arrived with the Europeans. Therefore, the Aztec had no milk or wool and no draft animals, that is, strong animals used to pull plows or carry heavy loads. Livestock on Aztec farms was primarily turkeys, ducks, and rabbits.

Aztec Women

Men were in charge of Aztec society. They made the laws, fought the wars, and were the head of the household. Men also did most of the work outside the home, in fields or workshops. Women spent most of their time in the home. They were expected to obey their husbands. But an Aztec woman did gain respect through motherhood.

Work in the Home

At home, women swept the house with brooms and looked after the children. Daily, they spent up to six hours grinding corn to make **tortillas** *(tawr TEE yuhz)* and other food. They went to the local market to buy food. They spun fibers and wove it into cloth. The sale of cloth was an important source of income.

Women played an important part in religious worship. They took food to the local temple to offer to the gods. In addition, every home had a little shrine (an object or place where people worshiped the gods). It was the woman's job to look after the shrine and to burn a sweet-smelling substance called **copal** *(KOH pal)* there.

Marriage and Childbirth

Many Aztec girls married when they were as young as 12. There were strict rules concerning the wedding. On the day before the ceremony, the bride's parents held a grand feast. The wedding itself took place the next evening. The bride dressed in red feathers and special clothes, and an old woman then carried her to her new home.

▶ A stone statue of Chalchiuhtlicue *(CHAHL chee oot LEE koo ay)*, the Aztec goddess of fresh water and of babies and marriage.

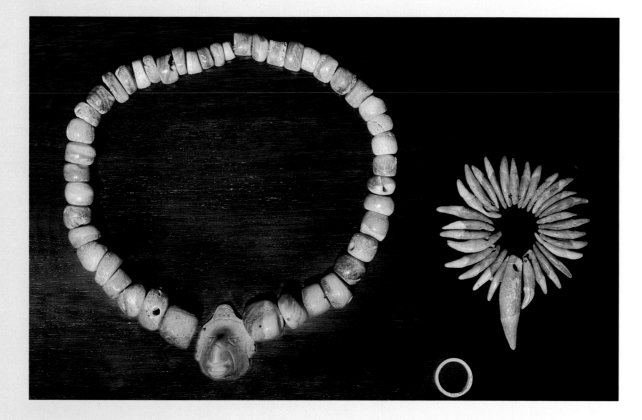

▲ Aztec jewelry, such as this necklace and bracelet made from stone beads, was worn only by **nobles.** Jewelry for both women and men was fashioned from gold, silver, such stones as **turquoise** and alabaster *(AL uh BAS tuhr)*, shell, clay, and wood.

The Aztec believed that special goddesses protected women who were giving birth. One of the goddesses protecting newborn babies was Ayopechcatl *(ah yoh PETCH kat uhl)*. When a woman was having a baby, a midwife, a woman who helps women in childbirth, came to the house to look after her. After the birth, if the child was a girl, the midwife buried the umbilical *(uhm BIHL uh kuhl)* cord, which connected the newborn baby to its mother, in the house. The midwife usually buried the cord for a girl child under the floor or under the stone used for grinding corn, to signify a daughter's attachment to the home.

An Aztec woman who died in childbirth was given the same respect as a warrior who died in battle. The Aztec believed that both warriors who died in battle and women who died in childbirth would, instead of going to the underworld, rise to the sun god Tonatiuh *(toh nah TEE wah)*.

A PREGNANT WOMAN'S PRAYER

Down there, where Ayopechcatl lives,
The jewel is born, a child has come into the world.
It is down there, in her own place, that the children are born.
Come, come here, new-born child, come here.
Come, come here, jewel child, come here.

A prayer to Ayopechcatl

SLAVES

At the bottom of the Aztec **social class** system were slaves, who worked for the person that owned them. The male slaves worked in the fields or as servants in the house. The female slaves wove cloth, made clothing, or prepared food. Slaves were not paid for this labor, but they were given food, shelter, and clothing.

Becoming a Slave

There were many ways of becoming enslaved in Aztec culture. Many of the prisoners captured by the Aztec in battle were offered up for sacrifice. But those who were not sacrificed might become slaves. Other slaves were foreigners seized by traders from other countries. The Aztec rulers forced many defeated states to send them slaves as **tribute**.

Aztec citizens could become slaves as well. Slavery was used as a punishment for many types of crimes, including robbery, kidnapping, and plotting against the **tlatoani** (*TLAH toh AH nee*). Many people also sold themselves into slavery to pay off a debt. Poor families sometimes sold one or more of their children into slavery.

The Rights of a Slave

Slaves who were Aztec had some rights. They were allowed to own land, and they could marry free citizens if they wished. Children born to one freeborn parent were themselves freeborn and not slaves. One of the greatest Aztec tlatoani, Itzcoatl (*eets koh AHT uhl*), was born to a mother who was a slave.

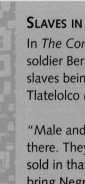

▶ A statue of the monkey, Ozomatli (*oh zoh MAHT lee*), who was believed to be the companion and servant of Xochipilli (*shoh chee PEE lee*), the Aztec god of flowers, plants, music, and dance.

Those who had been sold into slavery or who had entered into slavery to pay a debt could improve their position. If these slaves were able to save enough, they could buy back their freedom from their owner. They might also be set free when their master died or on the orders of the tlatoani.

▲ A sculpture created in the 1800's by the Mexican artist Jesus Contreras *(hay ZOOS kon TRAIR ehz)* depicts Itzcoatl, one of the greatest tlatoani. Itzcoatl, who ruled between 1426 and 1440, was born of a mother who was a slave.

CRIME AND PUNISHMENT

Aztec society was based on obedience to the law, and anyone who committed a crime was punished severely. Because the **tlatoani** *(TLAH toh AH nee)* himself had made all the laws, a person who broke a law was seen as having disobeyed the tlatoani. A **noble** who committed a crime was often punished more harshly than a commoner.

Laws covered every part of Aztec life. These included religion, public behavior, marriage, families, and property or possessions inherited from someone who died. However, one of the most important areas of law was the **social class** system. When Montezuma I introduced his new legal code in the 1440's, his main aim was to codify (organize legally) the gap between nobles and commoners.

▲ A caged prisoner cries, perhaps in humiliation, as passers-by point out his condition, in an illustration from the *Florentine Codex*.

▲ Aztec judges sentence criminals to death, by strangling (center top) and by beating (center bottom), in another illustration from the *Florentine Codex.*

The Law Courts

Each town or big village had its own law court. The judge was usually a senior soldier or local noble. He dealt with the less serious cases in the neighborhood; more serious cases went to courts in the large towns.

If people were not happy with the result of their case, they could appeal to the supreme council in Texcoco *(taysh KOH koh)*, which was made up of 12 judges. The judges had 80 days to make their decision. After this time, the case could go to two even higher judges, who consulted with the tlatoani. A ruling from this court was final.

Punishments

The Aztec had no prisons. People who were found guilty of serious crimes were put to death, usually by stoning or beating. Lesser punishments included destroying a person's house, taking away his property, or shaving his head.

The Aztec looked upon theft as one of the worst of all crimes. Robbery was rare, even though most homes had no doors or locks. Anyone who stole a person's crops or other property would be harshly punished. For example, the thief might become his victim's slave for a fixed period. In the worst cases, the thief might be condemned to death by strangling.

BELIEFS AND GODS

The Aztec had many stories about the creation of the world and the people in it. One story explained how the sun was created. One of the gods threw himself into a fire as a sacrifice and then rose out of the fire as the sun. However, he could not move unless other gods gave their blood, so they too burned on the fire, and the sun was able to move around the sky.

This **myth** shows how Aztec religion was based on the idea of sacrifice. As the gods had willingly burned themselves, humans had to repay them for this sacrifice with their own blood. If they failed to do this, the sun might stop moving and disaster would follow.

▶ The Aztec god Tlaloc is depicted in this wooden carving. As the god of rain, Tlaloc was important to the Aztec.

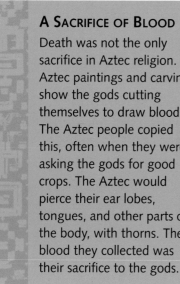

A SACRIFICE OF BLOOD

Death was not the only sacrifice in Aztec religion. Aztec paintings and carvings show the gods cutting themselves to draw blood. The Aztec people copied this, often when they were asking the gods for good crops. The Aztec would pierce their ear lobes, tongues, and other parts of the body, with thorns. The blood they collected was their sacrifice to the gods.

The Five Suns

The Aztec believed that there had been five ages, or "suns," in the history of the world. A different god had ruled the four ages, each of which was ended by a disaster. The sun was then reborn each time.

During the first sun, giants had lived on Earth, but jaguars had eaten Earth and the giants. Humans appeared during the second sun. Violent storms destroyed their world, and the people were turned into monkeys. The third sun was split apart by rain and fire, and the people turned into dogs, turkeys, and butterflies. Floods destroyed the fourth sun, and the people became fish. The Aztec believed they were living in the age of the fifth sun.

Gods and Goddesses

The Aztec worshiped many gods and goddesses. Each of these ruled some part of daily life. Among the most important gods and goddesses were—
• Huitzilopochtli *(WEE tsee loh POHCH tlee)*—god of war and protector of the Aztec
• Quetzalcoatl *(kehts ahl KOH ah tuhl)*—god of learning and of the wind
• Tlaloc *(TLAH lohk)*—god of rain, water, and fertility
• Coatlicue *(koh aht LEE kway)*—goddess of Earth and the mother of Huitzilopochtli
• Teteoinnan *(TAY tay oh EEN nahn)*, also called Toci *(TOHK ee)*—goddess of fertility and healing
• Tezcatlipoca *(tays KOHT lee POH kah)*—god of the night and all material things
• Tonatiuh *(toh nah TEE wah)*—fifth sun god and in charge of the Aztec heaven

▼ An image of the god Huitzilopochtli from the *Codex Magliabecchiano (mahg lee uh BEHK ee AHN oh)*, created in the mid-1500's. The Aztec believed that Huitzilopochtli had helped to create the earth and all the people on it. He was a powerful war god who needed a constant supply of victims sacrificed to him.

CEREMONIES AND HUMAN SACRIFICE

The Aztec held regular religious ceremonies during the year. Some were great public events, with a big audience of **nobles** and common people. Some were smaller ceremonies, where only priests and nobles were present in the local temple. The purpose of many of these ceremonies was to pray for **fertile** land and good harvests.

Ceremonies also took place in Aztec homes. Every household had a domestic shrine, which usually held clay figures of the gods, as well as pans for burning **copal** *(COH pal)*. Women looked after the shrines, making loaves of dough as offerings for the gods.

▲ A handle from an Aztec sacrificial knife, dating from the early 1500's, is decorated with mosaic made from pieces of **turquoise** and shell. It is in the form of a kneeling human figure, whose arms are embracing the point where the knife blade was fixed.

Heart Sacrifice

At the center of most major religious ceremonies was human sacrifice. Thousands of victims died every year in the temples. A sacrifice was a dramatic and shocking event, which was probably intended to show the power of the gods and the **tlatoani** *(TLAH toh AH nee)*.

One common way that sacrificial victims were killed was through removal of the heart. The priests took the victim to the temple, which was on a **pyramid** at the top of a giant flight of steps. They laid the person on a special stone and cut open his or her chest with a knife. A priest pulled out the victim's heart, as an offering to the sun. Then the victim was rolled down the steps to the bottom.

▼ An image from the *Codex Magliabecchiano,* created in the mid-1500's, shows how victims were sacrificed in an Aztec temple. Armed with an **obsidian** knife, the priest cut out the victim's heart, then sent the corpse rolling down the steep pyramid steps, leaving a trail of blood. Another priest cut off the head and set it on the skull rack.

Who Were the Victims?

Aztec priests used different types of victims for certain ceremonies. One important feast called for the sacrifice of an elderly noblewoman. Ceremonies for the rain gods required children. During an eclipse of the sun (a period when the moon passes between the sun and Earth, blocking the sun's light), albinos—who had pale skin, eyes, and hair—were sacrificed. The Aztec believed albinos were full of light.

Most sacrifice victims, however, were enemies captured in battle. Before the sacrifice, the Aztec treated these victims well, giving them fine food and other gifts, because they believed they were messengers who were going to the gods. Before the ceremony, they bathed the victims and dressed them in specially decorated robes.

INSIDE THE GREAT TEMPLE

In *The Conquest of New Spain,* Spanish soldier Bernal Díaz del Castillo describes the interior of Templo Mayor in Tenochtitlan *(tay nohch TEE tlahn):*

"There were some smoking braziers [fires]…in which they were burning the hearts of three Indians whom they had sacrificed that day; and all the walls of their shrine were so splashed and caked with blood that they and the floor too were black."

TEMPLES AND PRIESTS

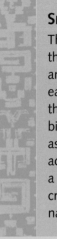

◀ A life-sized terra-cotta (baked clay) figure of a seated priest from the Totonac *(teh TAHN ihk)* culture, a people who were absorbed into the Aztec empire.

Most ceremonies and other religious events took place inside special buildings. Even the smallest village usually had a local temple. The big cities had grander temples, often built at the top of a huge **pyramid.** The most magnificent of all was the Templo Mayor in Tenochtitlan *(tay nohch TEE tlahn).*

Inside the temples were statues of the gods. Priests, who lived in rooms in the center of the temple, looked after the temples and led the daily worship of the gods. The priests also studied the sky at sunrise, sunset, and midnight. By watching the movements of stars, clouds, and even birds, they believed they could foretell the future.

Training To Be a Priest

Boys of the **noble** class went to **calmecac** *(KAHL may KAHK)*, a school run by priests. Some of these young boys might decide to study to become priests when they grew up. Commoner boys could also train for the priesthood if they showed special promise. These boys in training were known as "little priests." They learned about Aztec religion and the duties of a priest.

At about the age of 20, a "little priest" might make a firm decision to become a priest. This meant he would not be able to marry, and he would become a full priest for life. Only some priests rose to the position of fire priest, or "fire seller." They performed the human sacrifices.

Daily Duties

The main job of the ordinary priest was to perform the daily **rituals** in the temple. Priests had to keep the sacred fires burning, and they had to burn **copal** *(COH pal)*. They also had to make offerings of food to the gods (though they usually then ate this food themselves).

Priests organized the running of the temple. This might include work on a temple or cleaning and taking care of the temple treasures. Priests also taught in the calmecac and helped in the training of new priests. Unlike the vast majority of the Aztec, priests could read and write, so they kept records of daily events.

▼ A stone statue known as a chac mool *(chawk mool)* from the sanctuary of the rain god, Tlaloc *(TLAH lohk)*, at the Templo Mayor in present-day Mexico City, believed to represent a messenger to the gods. Chac mools are always lying down, with their heads turned and legs drawn up. A dish, possibly used for holding blood or other offerings, rests on their stomachs.

THE AZTEC CALENDAR

The Aztec took their ideas about time from the Maya and other **Mesoamerican** peoples before them. The Aztec believed that time was something sacred. Different gods were thought to guard the days, the months, the years, and even the centuries. People also believed that the gods controlled time.

For this reason, it is not surprising that the Aztec were very interested in the passing of time. They even had two different kinds of calendars. They used these calendars to record important moments in the year and to help them mark out what would happen in the future.

▼ Part of an Aztec calendar from the *Codex Cospi (coh spee)*, created by the Mixtec *(MEESH tehk)* culture between 1350 to 1500. Because the Aztec believed time was controlled by the gods and was, thus, sacred, calendars were central to the lives of the people.

The Ordinary Calendar

The ordinary Aztec calendar had 365 days, as does our calendar. It was divided into 18 months, each of which had 20 days. A month was divided into 4 weeks, which each had 5 days. That left 5 extra days at the end of the year, which the Aztec thought were unlucky days.

This calendar set out the dates for ordinary events. It included the correct times for planting and harvesting crops, as well as for regular ceremonies. It showed that large markets took place every five days. Smaller ones took place only once a month.

The Religious Calendar

The religious calendar used by the Aztec was very different from their ordinary calendar. It had 260 days divided into 13 months. Each of these months had 20 days, and each of the 20 days had a different name. These were mostly animal names, and they included alligator, lizard, snake, jaguar, and vulture.

Because the religious calendar was shorter, the years for the two calendars did not usually end at the same time. Only once every 52 years did the 2 calendars end on the same day. This important day was marked by the Binding of the Years, or the New Fire Ceremony. The Aztec put out the central fire in the hearth of their homes. Priests then lit a fire on the chest of a sacrificial victim. This fire was taken to towns and cities throughout the empire. Then the people relit their hearth fires from the new fire and feasted to show they had started a new era.

▲ An Aztec stone carving representing the bundle of sticks, bound with rope at either end, that was used in the festival and feast day known as the Binding of the Years. On that day, people put out their hearth fires, and priests ignited a bundle of 52 sticks on the chest of a human sacrifice. Flames from the fire were carried throughout the empire to relight hearth fires

THE SACRED NUMBER
The number 13 represented gods and goddesses in the Aztec religious calendar. This calendar had a cycle of 13 months, which was repeated throughout the year. The Aztec believed one of their gods or goddesses ruled each month.

THE GREAT CITY OF TENOCHTITLAN

By the early 1500's, Tenochtitlan *(tay nohch TEE tlahn)* was one of the world's most magnificent cities, with beautiful stone **pyramids,** palaces, marketplaces, and canals. Because of its many canals, in fact, the Spanish considered Tenochtitlan to be the Venice of the New World.

Tenochtitlan had spread and swallowed up Tlatelolco *(TLAH tay LOHL koh)*, its rival town to the north. Around Tenochtitlan were other cities on the lake and on the shore. About 200,000 people lived in the city of Tenochtitlan and the surrounding area.

How the City Was Built

When the Aztec first arrived at Lake Texcoco *(taysh KOH koh)* in about 1325, the island on which Tenochtitlan stood was mud and swamp. As the empire grew stronger, the capital city grew bigger. The Aztec joined several small islands to form one large one, covering more than 5 square miles (13 square kilometers).

The streets in Tenochtitlan ran either north to south or east to west and formed squares, or blocks. The three widest streets joined with **causeways**, which connected Tenochtitlan with the shore. Drinking water from the highlands flowed into the city along two big **aqueducts** *(AK wuh duhktz)*—artificial channels through which water is taken to the place where it is used.

◀ An artist's rendering of the Templo Mayor at the center of Tenochtitlan at the height of the Aztec empire.

The Temples

At the center of Tenochtitlan stood the main religious buildings. These were the temples to the most important gods, as well as the **calmecac** (*KAHL may KAHK*) and the rack where priests hung the skulls of victims. Around the buildings was the Serpent Wall, which was decorated with huge carvings of snakes' heads.

The tallest and most splendid building was the Great Temple pyramid, the Templo Mayor. Two giant staircases ran up the west side of the pyramid, stained with blood from sacrifices. On the top were shrines to the two most important gods, Tlaloc *(TLAH lohk)*, the god of rain, and Huitzilopochtli *(WEE tsee loh POHCH tlee)*, the god of war. In front of each shrine was a sacrificial stone.

Remains of this temple have been found beneath current-day Mexico City. **Archaeologists** study these remains to learn more about Aztec culture.

▶ A modern view of the Templo Mayor site in Mexico City. The site was discovered in 1978 by workers digging a new sewer. The temple is still being excavated by archaeologists.

PYRAMID CONSTRUCTION

The pyramids were built to represent the mountains, which the Aztec believed to be the home of their ancestors. These pyramids were used as temples. The inside of a pyramid was usually painted and decorated.

After a pyramid was built, it was often made larger and grander to honor the gods. Often, the Aztec would build a larger pyramid over an existing pyramid. When archaeologists began excavating the Templo Mayor, they discovered it had been rebuilt at least seven times—each time on top of the earlier pyramid—and enlarged many more times.

Because the land beneath Tenochtitlan was swampy, any large, heavy building in the city was always sinking. The new layers of temples helped to keep the sinking pyramid tall and impressive.

LANGUAGE AND WRITING

The Aztec spoke a language called Nahuatl *(NAH wah tuhl)*. This belongs to a group of languages that includes those spoken by the Comanche *(kuh MAN chee)*, Shoshone *(shoh SHOH nee)*, and some other American Indian peoples. By the 1500's, Nahuatl had become the most important language in **Mesoamerica.**

Writing in Pictures

The Aztec did not have an alphabet, so they could not write down their language in letters. Instead they used small pictures, called **glyphs** *(glihfz),* which were often colored. The color added meaning to the glyph. For example, the color of a glyph used to show a person's name also told their rank. Glyphs for the name of a ruler always contained the color turquoise.

In Aztec writing, some glyphs stood for ideas, while others stood for syllables (the sounds that make up a word). Both kinds of glyphs could be combined to show a word. For example, the pictures for the

AZTEC POETRY

With flowers you paint,
O Giver of Life!
With songs you give color,
With songs you shade
Those who will live on Earth.
Later you will destroy eagles and jaguars:
We live only in your painting
Here, on Earth.
With black ink you will blot out
All that was friendship,
Brotherhood, nobility.
You give shading
To those who will live on Earth.
We live only in your book of paintings,
Here on Earth.

A chant the Aztec sang of one of the gods

▼ Aztec codices, or books—such as the *Codex Fejervary-Mayer,* shown partially unfolded—are one of the most important sources of information about the world of the Aztec. The glyphs in the *Codex Fejervary-Mayer* were painted on dried deerskin washed with lime.

Aztec town of Coatepec *(koh ah TAY payk)* were a snake and a hill. The Nahuatl words for "snake" and "hill" were "coatl" *(koh AHT uhl)* and "tepetl" *(tay PEHY tuhl)*, respectively. These two words together sounded almost like Coatepec.

Scribes and Books

Writing was done by specially trained craftsmen called **scribes**. These scribes were usually members of the upper class, but sometimes a scribe might be a commoner who worked for a **noble** or a priest. Aztec scribes wrote records of history, religion, and daily events. A scribe worked with charcoal and inks that he made himself.

The Aztec produced a kind of paper made from tree bark. They also wrote on animal skins or on woven cloth. They folded a long strip of paper back and forth to form the pages of a kind of book called a **codex**. The codex usually had a wooden board, a book cover, at each end to protect the pages.

A few Aztec codices (*KOH deh seez* —the plural for codex) exist today. Many of them are in important libraries around the world.

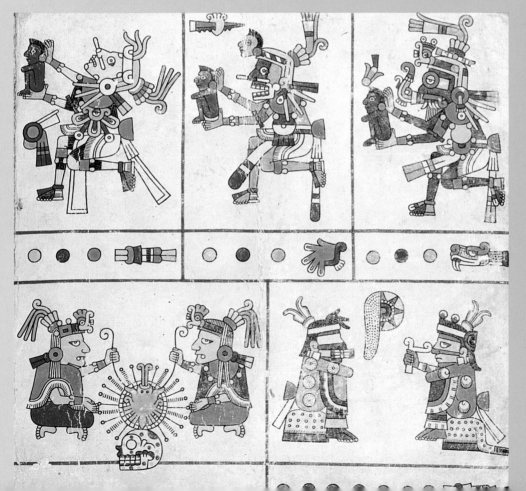

◀ A page from the *Codex Fejervary-Mayer*, which is in the collection of the Liverpool Museum in the United Kingdom, illustrates **rituals** involving a newborn child and scenes of various human behaviors.

AZTEC ART AND CRAFTS

Artists and craftsmen had a special place in the commoner class. In Aztec society, they ranked just below the merchants. The artists produced sculptures and paintings on religious subjects. These works decorated temples, shrines, and palaces. The craftsmen made such goods as pots, jars, tools, ropes, and clothing, which were vital for everyday life.

Sculptures

Aztec sculptors created all kinds of carvings from stone. Many of them worked for the **tlatoani** *(TLAH toh AH nee)* and senior **nobles,** for whom they made giant, dramatically detailed figures. The carvings made by Aztec sculptors included

▼ A great Sun Stone has the face of the sun god Tonatiuh crying out for blood sacrifice. He is encircled by symbols of the earthquake that will destroy the world; then by signs of the days and months of the year. The original stone was uncovered in the ruins of the Templo Mayor **pyramid** in present-day Mexico City.

statues of the gods in the temples of **Tenochtitlan** *(tay nohch TEE tlahn)* and large ceremonial stones such as the Sun Stone, sometimes called the Calendar Stone. This stone is about 12 feet (3.7 meters) in diameter. At its center is the face of the sun god Tonatiuh *(toh nah TEE wah)*. Other carvings represent the days of the Aztec month and religious symbols related to the sun god.

These grand carvings were intended to show the power of the tlatoani and of the Aztec armies. Other sculptors produced smaller god figures and models of temples for private shrines in the homes of nobles and rich commoners. Statues also showed animals, such as jaguars, snakes, and dogs, and much smaller creatures, such as fleas and frogs.

The Other Crafts

Some Aztec craftsmen made luxury items, such as headdresses and mats from the feathers of the rare quetzal *(keht SAHL)*, a large bird with beautiful tail feathers. Other luxury craftsmen made masks and jewelry from **jade, turquoise,** and precious stones.

Smiths worked in gold and silver, and herbalists *(UR buh lihstz)* made medicines from plants. Other craftsmen included carpenters and potters.

▲ An ornament, made of turquoise, wood, and shell, in the shape of a double-headed snake. The snake's open jaws represent the entrance to the underworld. Priests wore such magnificent pectoral (chest) ornaments as this during major ceremonies.

MIRROR OF THE GODS

One of the items made by Aztec craftsmen were mirrors. The Aztec made their mirrors from **obsidian**. They treated mirrors as magical and holy objects. The Aztec believed that the god Tezcatlipoca *(tays KOHT lee POH kah)* always carried a mirror of polished gold. When an Aztec person saw his or her reflection in a mirror, he or she believed it showed them that Tezcatlipoca was watching everything that happened in the world. In fact, the Aztec name for a mirror meant "place from which he watches."

FAMILY LIFE

There were about six family members living together in most Aztec households. In a usual household, a husband and wife lived with their unmarried children and several of the husband's relatives. Sometimes, two married couples from the same family shared a house.

Family life for Aztec commoners mostly consisted of long hours of labor, either in the home or in the fields. There were days off for religious ceremonies and other festivals. People from all levels of society tried to follow the same standards of behavior—they were expected to be obedient, honest, and hardworking.

A Family's Day

The family got up when the sun rose, and they washed in a nearby pond or lake. The women of the house started the fire on the hearth stones, then they began grinding the corn into flour. Later, they used this flour to make the family's meal. Meanwhile, the men went out into their fields or workshops.

Everybody stopped work to eat at midday. This was the main meal of the day. They might have a short sleep after their meal, before returning to their labor. Work only ended when the sun went down. The Aztec went to bed early, soon after dark.

AZTEC DOGS

The Aztec had great respect for dogs. They liked dogs because they were loyal and protected homes and crops. Craftsmen made many carvings of dogs. There are also several pet names for dogs in Nahuatl *(NAH wah tuhl)*, including "chichi" *(chee chee)* and "tehui" *(teh WEE)*. However, the Aztec also ate dog meat for which they raised a special breed of small dogs.

◄ A model of the interior of a one-room Aztec house, on display at the National Museum of Anthropology in Mexico City, shows objects of everyday use. The hearth, in the center, consists of three stones supporting the comal *(ko MAHL)*, a clay disc on which the women cooked **tortillas** *(tawr TEE yuhz)*. The family would have slept on reed mats, rolled up during the day.

Living Outside

Houses were often clustered together in groups of between two and five. The families who lived in a group of houses shared a yard. They kept the yard clear by putting what little trash they generated at the sides or rear of the houses. Many Aztec homes were small. Because the climate of the area is fairly warm, people spent much of their time outside.

Gardens were important to the Aztec. People grew flowers as well as vegetables in their yard or on their roof. In the country, they raised a few animals. Some animals, such as turkeys and rabbits, were for eating, but others, such as macaws *(muh KAWZ)* and parrots, were kept as pets.

▼A member of the Aztec nobility accompanies his sons to a temple school in a drawing from the *Florentine Codex*.

SHELTER AND CLOTHING

Most Aztec houses were made of **adobe** (*uh DOH bee*), or sun-dried bricks. The homes of most Aztec were all the same design. They had only one room that was divided into four areas. Each home had a sleeping area, a kitchen where food was prepared, a small shrine, and a main living area. Many families also had a separate bathhouse.

Wealthy Aztec had much larger homes, which were sometimes made of stone. These homes were sometimes more than one story high, and some stood on raised platforms. Of course, the **tlatoani** *(TLAH toh AH nee)* had the biggest house of all. One of the royal palaces had 300 rooms, including a council chamber and law courts. Its huge gardens contained fountains, a **maze,** and a zoo.

Furniture

Most Aztec slept on one or more mats on the floor. To make a seat, they put a mat on a low mound of earth or a wooden frame, but most people sat cross-legged on a cushion. People kept clothes (and other valuable objects) in baskets with lids.

▲ A scene depicting the inside of an Aztec house, taken from the *Florentine Codex*, a manuscript compiled in about 1570. Aztec women spent much of the day preparing food and offering **copal** *(KOH pal)* to the gods.

The houses of poor people had plain, whitewashed walls and earthen floors. Wealthier people decorated their walls with paintings or colored cloths. Their houses might also have floors of wood or stone.

Clothes

Aztec men wore a loincloth—a cloth wrapped around their waist and between their legs. Above this, they wore a cape knotted over the right shoulder. Women wore a skirt, wrapped around the waist and tied with a belt, and a sleeveless blouse.

Most people had to make their clothes from cheap, coarse materials. The most common cloth was made from the fibers of the **maguey** plant. Workers cut the plant's leaves, scraped away the flesh from the leaves, and dried the leaves in the sun. Then they pulled out the long fibers and spun them together into yarn for weaving.

▼ Images from the *Florentine Codex* provide a glimpse of the clothing worn by the Aztec. A woman (left) is shown in a long skirt and a loose blouse. A man (right) wears a cloak fastened on one shoulder. The couple were almost certainly nobles because both are wearing colored clothing and jewelry and have on a kind of sandal.

DRESS CODE

There were strict laws about clothing:

- Commoners wore simple clothing with little or no decoration.
- **Nobles** could wear cotton garments. These garments might be decorated with patterns and colors, fringes, and feathers.
- Priests wore black or dark green cloaks. These were often decorated with pictures of human bones and skulls.
- Only Aztec rulers and high-ranking priests and nobles could wear **turquoise** ornaments.

FOOD AND DRINK

Corn was the main ingredient of most Aztec dishes. For their first meal of the day, they usually ate cornmeal porridge (a hot cereal) sweetened with honey. At midday and in the evening, workers often ate flat cornmeal pancakes, which we now call **tortillas** *(tawr TEE yuhz)*. Sometimes they ate **tamales** (tah MAH leez).

Aztec farmers grew many kinds of vegetables and fruits on their **chinampas** *(chee NAHM pahs)*. Beans, tomatoes, squash, and chili peppers were the most common. Most Aztec ate little meat. Typically, the only animals raised for food were turkeys, ducks, rabbits, and a special breed of small dogs (different from the dogs they kept as pets).

The Aztec caught wild birds and animals, as well as fish and frogs. They sold many of these, along with their own produce, in the city markets. The Aztec also collected and ate insects—including ants and grasshoppers—worms, and a blue-green algae (simple, one-celled life forms), which they gathered in nets from lakes.

The Food of the Rich

Aztec **nobles** had a much grander diet than ordinary people. Grandest of all was the food served to Montezuma II. Every day his cooks prepared more than 300 different dishes, from which he would choose. There were dishes made from fruits and vegetables, and items featuring duck, rabbit, crow, and pigeon.

▶ The *Florentine Codex* includes these images of Aztec women preparing a feast or banquet.

While eating, Montezuma sat at a low table covered with a white cloth. Because the **tlatoani** *(TLAH toh AH nee)* was considered to be a god, servants set up a golden screen so that no one could see him eating. The Spanish told stories of Montezuma drinking chocolate after his meal from cups made of solid gold.

What Did the Aztec Drink?

Most Aztec usually drank water. Their only alcoholic drink was a beverage called **octli** *(OHK tlee)*, or pulque *(POOL kay)*. This drink was made from the juice of the **maguey** plant. The Aztec drank octli only on such special occasions as festivals or religious ceremonies. There were harsh punishments (even including death) for someone who became drunk.

FROM WHERE DID CHOCOLATE COME?

Chocolate was a very popular drink for some Aztec. It was made from the beans of the cacao plant, which came from the hot regions near the coast. However, it was very expensive and only wealthy people could afford to drink it. Cacao beans became so valuable that Aztec merchants used them as a form of money.

◀ A stone cocoa jug carved in the shape of a hare. Nobles drank the cocoa directly from the jug with straws, some made of gold. Cocoa was made by grinding cacao beans and mixing the powder with water and a kind of gum.

CHILDREN AND EDUCATION

The birth of a child was a time for celebrating, when family and friends came to greet the baby and give presents. The parents talked with a priest, who helped them choose the child's name. At dawn the next day, the midwife who had assisted at the baby's birth announced that name.

The parents gave their child a special gift. If the baby was a boy, they gave him a little shield, a bow, and four arrows. These were symbols that the baby would grow up to be a warrior. If the baby was a girl, the parents gave her a brush, a basket, and a spindle (a tool for spinning thread). These showed that she would grow up to be a housewife.

Schooling at Home

Aztec children began their education at home, until about the age of 15, but boys and girls were treated very differently. The father educated his son. He taught him how to handle a canoe, how to catch fish, and other skills. The mother educated her daughter. She taught her how to spin thread, how to sweep the floors, and how to grind corn.

Parents educated their boys and girls to be obedient and well behaved. Children who were lazy or naughty received harsh punishments. Their parents might beat them or scratch them with thorns. Parents might even make their children breathe in the smoke from burning chili peppers, which stung the eyes and throats.

▲ The Aztec believed the god Ixtilton *(eez TLIHL tuhn)*, pictured here in the form of an **obsidian** mask, watched over children in their beds and helped them sleep peacefully.

At School

Most boys went to the local school, called the **telpochcalli** *(TEL potch CAL ley)*, which means "house of the young men." Here, boys learned about being warriors and how to build roads and repair canals. Most daughters stayed in the home. They were taught how to cook, how to make cloth and other household items, and how to run the household. Boys from **noble** or wealthy families usually went to a **calmecac** *(KAHL may KAHK)*, or religious school. They were trained to become priests or government officials.

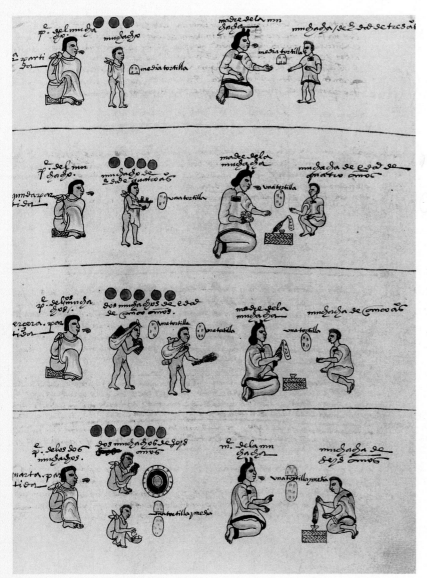

◀ Aztec parents training their children, shown in the *Codex Mendoza (mehn DOH zuh),* from the mid-1500's. A father (left column) teaches his son such skills as carrying goods. A mother (right column) teaches her daughter spinning.

SPORTS AND FESTIVALS

▲ Small Aztec flutes made of clay. The Aztec used music at festivals and in religious ceremonies.

The Aztec loved all kinds of sports and games. **Nobles** enjoyed hunting wild birds in parks or large gardens. Their main weapons were blowpipes (tubes through which a person blows darts or other objects). The Aztec used blowpipes to shoot tiny clay balls.

Once a year, there was a grand hunt meeting in the countryside near Tlatelolco *(TLAH tay LOHL koh)*. A long line of warriors moved across the hills, driving out deer, coyote, and rabbits to be killed.

Commoners had simpler amusements. One of their favorite games was **patolli** *(pah TOHL lee)*. This was played on a board divided into squares. The players threw beans marked with dots

AZTEC MUSICAL INSTRUMENTS

Music was an important part of Aztec festivals.

• Drums were usually made of wood and covered with jaguar skin. Musicians played the drums with their hands.

• Gongs were made of wood, stone, or metal and were hit with mallets.

• Flutes were made from clay. Some were in the shape of birds, such as the macaw—a kind of parrot.

• Conch *(konch)* shells were cut open and blown like a horn.

• Rattles were made of dried seed pods or clay vessels filled with little stones.

(similar to dice), moved colored stones across the squares, and made bets about who would win. Some people lost so much money by gambling at patolli that they had to sell themselves as slaves to pay the debt.

The Ball Game

The most popular Aztec sport was the ball game they called **ullamaliztli** *(OOL lah mah LEES tlee)*. The people of **Mesoamerica** had played this for many centuries. The game took place between two teams in an I-shaped, walled court. There was a carved stone ring on each side wall of the court.

The aim of the game was to put a heavy rubber ball through one of the rings. This must have been very difficult since the players were only allowed to touch the ball with their knees or hips. When a team scored a "goal" through a ring, they won the game.

Festivals

Each month had its own religious festival. In the dry month of April, for example, there was a special ceremony in which the people begged the gods for rain to help the crops. There were human sacrifices and dances by men and women. Priests carried an image of Huitzilopochtli *(WEE tsee loh POHCH tlee)*, the god of war and the supreme god of the Aztec, through the streets.

Another important ceremony was the Great Feast of the Dead, which lasted for a month in late summer. People celebrated the lives of their dead ancestors by displaying the ancestor's skulls and bones and holding feasts. The Mexican holiday that honors the dead—the Day of the Dead, or Día de los muertos *(DEE ah deh lohs MWEHR tohs)*—is in some ways similar to this Aztec festival.

▼ The *Codex Borbonicus, (bohr BON ih kehs)* made sometime before 1521, illustrates an Aztec ball court used for the game of ullamaliztli.

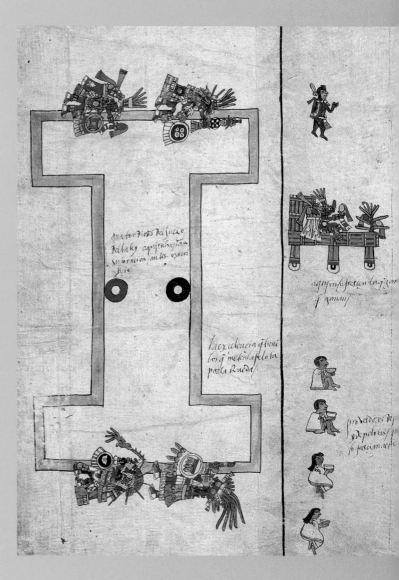

TRADE AND TRANSPORTATION

Trade with other lands was vital to the Aztec. They needed raw materials and other goods that they could not produce themselves. In exchange, they sent their own produce to other regions.

As the Aztec empire grew stronger and bigger, goods of all kinds flowed into Tenochtitlan *(tay nohch TEE tlahn)* and Tlatelolco *(TLAH tay LOHL koh)*. Farmers and craftsmen brought their crops and products to sell. Merchants arrived with their loads after traveling long distances. In addition, nations that had been conquered by the Aztec sent huge quantities of goods as **tribute**.

How Did the Markets Work?

Markets were the main places for buying and selling goods, and the grandest marketplace was in Tlatelolco. Here, people could buy almost anything produced in **Mesoamerica** and beyond. However, every town or village had

▼ Merchants sit in the marketplace with their goods laid out for sale in this image from the *Florentine Codex,* written and illustrated in the mid-1500's. The merchants are selling feathers, skins, jewelry, and richly woven cloth.

its own, smaller, trading site. Some places specialized in certain goods. For example, one town was famous for its timber, another for its chilies and honey, another for slaves.

Trading rules were very strict. The markets had their own police force patrolling the stalls. Anyone found breaking the rules was taken to a special court and punished. A trader who cheated a customer might be fined, and someone caught stealing might be beaten to death.

Transportation Without Wheels

The Aztec knew how wheels worked. They made clay toys with little wheels for their children to push along. However, they never used wheels for full-size carts or wagons. Such carts and wagons would have been of little use since the Aztec had no large domestic animals, such as oxen, horses, or mules, to pull them.

Human beings were, therefore, the main form of transportation. Huge numbers of people—called porters—carried goods over long and short distances. These porters played a very important part in the Aztec economy. The other kind of transportation was by water. The lakes and canals around Tenochtitlan were always busy with canoes and flat-bottomed boats carrying goods.

MAKING BOATS

The Aztec made boats out of two kinds of materials. They built rafts from bundles of reeds woven together. They also carved flat-bottomed boats from the trunks of trees, using copper or **obsidian** tools to hollow out the insides. Most boats were about 13 feet (4 meters) long. They could carry cargo or up to five people.

◀ Aztec porters carry a merchant's goods across country in an illustration from the *Florentine Codex*. The pack on a porter's back was attached with a long strap going around the forehead. The fact that the porters are wearing more than just loincloths reveals that the illustration was made after the 1521 Spanish conquest. Roman Catholic missionaries, who came to Mexico to convert the Aztec to Christianity, stressed modesty in their teachings.

DECLINE AND DANGER

▲ An illustration, from *Historia de las Indias (ih STOHR eeh uh day lahs IHN dee uhs)* from 1579, depicting Hernán Cortés meeting Aztec representatives of the tlatoani as he travels toward Tenochtitlan. The Aztec **nobles** present Cortés with rich gifts and an order that he is to turn around and leave.

By the early 1500's, the Aztec empire had reached its peak. The **tlatoani** *(TLAH toh AH nee)* ruled lands up to 620 miles (998 kilometers) away from Tenochtitlan *(tay nohch TEE tlahn)*, but the Aztec empire was now so big that it was difficult to control.

The Aztec also had many enemies. The conquered peoples hated the harsh rule under the Aztec, and they were tired of sending huge amounts of **tribute** to Tenochtitlan and providing victims for sacrifices. In 1515, the Aztec were defeated in battle by the forces of Tlaxcala *(teh lahs KAH lah)*, a city in the east. Soon afterward, there was a **drought** in the Valley of Mexico, which caused terrible **famine**.

TIMELINE OF THE SPANISH IN MESOAMERICA

1492 Christopher Columbus crosses the Atlantic and lands on San Salvador

1493-1504 Columbus makes three more voyages to Central America

1511 Spanish found colony on Cuba

1517 Francisco de Córdoba *(KOHR doh bah)* lands at Yucatán Peninsula

1518 Juan de Grijalva *(gree HAHL vah)* lands at Yucatán

1519 Hernán Cortés lands at Cape Catoche *(keh TOH cheh)* and marches inland

Invaders from Europe

Meanwhile, an even bigger threat had appeared. In 1492, the first Europeans reached the New World. They were Spaniards, led by the Italian Christopher Columbus. This first expedition landed in the West Indies. During the next 12 years, Columbus made three more voyages to the New World, exploring other islands and reaching the mainland coast.

More Spanish expeditions soon followed. The Europeans were excited by stories of gold and other treasures in the Americas. In 1517, a small force from Cuba landed on the Yucatán *(yoo kuh TAHN)* Peninsula—an area that included parts of present-day southeastern Mexico, northern Guatemala, and Belize. A year later, a second expedition explored the coast of what is now Mexico. Reports of the strangers were carried to Montezuma II.

▲ A map of Tenochtitlan, which may have been drawn by Hernán Cortés, clearly shows the Templo Mayor and other important buildings in the center. The white lines radiating out from the city represent **causeways** carrying roads over Lake Texcoco *(taysh KOH koh)* to the mainland.

The Arrival of Cortés

A third expedition sailed from Cuba under Hernán Cortés *(ehr NAHN kawr TEHZ)* in February 1519. Cortés had 11 ships, about 100 sailors, and 500 soldiers, armed with muskets and cannons.

Cortés set off inland toward Tenochtitlan. He knew his tiny force could not defeat an empire rumored to have 250,000 armed men. He needed allies, so he approached cautiously, either defeating or making friends with enemies of Montezuma II. By the time Cortés was nearing the capital city, he led an army of hundreds of Spaniards and thousands of Indians.

The Fall of the Aztec Empire

Montezuma II was alarmed when he got news about the new Spanish force. He sent messengers with rich gifts for Cortés and a message ordering the Spaniards to leave.

Cortés and his men were delighted with the gifts, which were made of gold and other precious materials. Now they were certain that Mexico was rich in treasures, and they marched on toward Tenochtitlan *(tay nohch TEE tlahn)*. By November 1519, Cortés and his forces reached Lake Texcoco *(taysh KOH koh)* and began crossing one of the **causeways**.

The Capture of Montezuma

Montezuma allowed the invaders to enter Tenochtitlan. He went out to welcome Cortés and took him to his palace. Here, Cortés seized Montezuma and held him as hostage to ensure the safety

▼ Cortés and his soldiers are shown attacking Tenochtitlan's Templo Mayor in this engraving from the *Lienzo* ("canvas") *de Tlaxcala (lee EHN zoh deh teh lahs KAH lah)*, made in about 1550.

ycq̃tla ti tetzaviitl
yn mal ques.

56

quintlatique.

▲ Roman Catholic friars (missionary monks) watch the execution of the Aztec who have refused to convert to Christianity, in a drawing in pen and ink from the *Lienzo de Tlaxcala*. The Spanish tried to stamp out all traces of the Aztec religion.

THE DEATH OF MONTEZUMA II

A Spanish soldier who served under Cortés, Bernal Díaz del Castillo, wrote of how Montezuma II died in the work *The Conquest of New Spain*. According to Díaz, Montezuma was killed by his own people:

"Montezuma was lifted to a battlement of the roof...and began to speak very lovingly to his people . . . Barely was this speech finished when a sudden shower of stones and darts descended . . . Montezuma was hit by three stones . . . and though they begged him to have his wounds dressed and eat some food . . . he refused. Then . . . we were told that he was dead."

The Aztec, however, claimed Montezuma was murdered by the Spaniards. No one really knows for certain how he died.

of his Spanish soldiers. The Spaniards began to take control, stealing the Aztec treasure and trying to stop their religious ceremonies.

In June 1520, the Aztec rose up against the Spanish forces. After a week of bitter fighting, the Spaniards tried to sneak out of the city, but the Aztec discovered them. Many Spaniards were killed, and Montezuma also died during the fighting. Cortés led his men to safety in nearby Tlaxcala *(teh lahs KAH lah)*.

Death and Destruction

In October, a **smallpox** epidemic broke out in Tenochtitlan. The Spaniards had brought the disease to the New World. People living in the Americas had never before encountered it and had no immunity (natural protection) for it. Smallpox devastated the Aztec empire. Thousands of Aztec died, and this weakened the empire and its ability to fight the Spaniards.

Cortés returned to Tenochtitlan in December with Spanish forces and a large army of Indians from lands previously conquered by the Aztec. By May 1521, he had surrounded the Aztec capital with his army and boats, and he had cut off the city's food and water supplies. Battles, sickness, and starvation weakened the Aztec army. In August, the new **tlatoani** *(TLAH toh AH nee)* surrendered the city.

Cortés sent soldiers to take over the rest of the Aztec empire. Some Indians resisted, but most accepted Spanish rule without a fight. The Spaniards went on to destroy many of the Aztec cities. They believed it was their duty as Christians to wipe out all traces of Aztec religion, which they believed was inspired by the devil. They destroyed Tenochtitlan and built Mexico City on the ruins.

THE AZTEC LEGACY

Today, few Aztec buildings still stand. The invaders removed the treasures and pulled down and buried over the stone statues and other remains. However, the Aztec **civilization** has not disappeared. **Archaeologists** have uncovered several major sites in which they have found a huge number of Aztec items.

Many modern Mexicans look back to the Aztec era with great pride. Thousands of people in Mexico and the United States have Aztec ancestors.

Digging Up the Past

The rediscovery of the Aztec began in 1790, when workers digging a sewer in Mexico City found a large statue of an Aztec goddess. A year later, they found the famous Sun Stone. The greatest find of all was the remains of the Templo Mayor **pyramid** in downtown Mexico City. In 1978, workers accidentally dug into the pyramid's long-buried foundations, where more than

AZTEC WORDS

People all over the world use ancient Nahuatl words without knowing it:

Avocado a fruit eaten mainly in dips and salads
Chili a spicy pepper
Chocolate
Cocoa
Coyote a small wolf-like animal living in western North America
Mesquite a tree
Ocelot a medium-sized animal of the cat family
Shack a hut
Tomato a fruit eaten like a vegetable

◀ A modern market in an Indian village in Chiapas *(chee AHP uhs)* State, Mexico, is very similar to the markets held by the Aztecs between the 1300's and 1500's.

6,000 objects, including jewelry, carvings, and the remains of human sacrifices, were eventually discovered built into the structure. Mexico City's many wonderful museums, including the National Museum of Anthropology and the Templo Mayor Museum, are treasure troves of Aztec artifacts.

▲ Women in Mexico cover a grave with flowers for the Day of the Dead. The celebration is similar to the ancient Aztec ceremony the Great Feast of the Dead.

The Aztec Today

Many Mexicans speak a modern version of Nahuatl *(NAH wah tuhl).* They eat chocolate, chilies, beans, and cornmeal **tortillas** *(tawr TEE yuhz),* all of which have Aztec origins. There are still vast open-air markets throughout Mexico, as there were during Aztec times.

There are many other reminders of the great Aztec empire. Many Mexican place names come from the Nahuatl language. These include Acapulco *(AH kah POOL koh)* and Mexico itself. Famous Mexican painters—such as 1900's painter Diego Rivera *(dee AY goh reh VAYR uh)*—have used Aztec themes in their work. Mexico's national symbol, which can be seen on the Mexican flag, is an eagle perched on a cactus and holding a snake. This image comes from the Aztec **legend** of the founding of Tenochtitlan *(tay nohch TEE tlahn)* long ago.

GLOSSARY

adobe Brick made of clay baked in the sun.

alliance A union formed by agreement, joining the interests of people or states.

aqueduct An artificial channel through which water is taken to the place where it will be used.

archaeologist A scientist who studies the remains of past human cultures.

atlatl A spear-throwing device once used by many Indian groups.

calmecac A religious school run by Aztec priests.

calpolli A group of Aztec families that lived together in a neighborhood and shared a plot of land.

causeway A raised road or path, usually built across swampy, wet ground or shallow water.

chinampa An area of a shallow lake made into farmland by scooping up mud from the lake bottom to form an island.

civilization The way of life in a society that features complex economic, governmental, and social systems.

codex An early book (plural, codices). Some of the codices of the Aztec were made before 1521 and feature only **glyphs** and pictures. Other codices, made after the Spanish arrived, also have text in Spanish and Nahuatl (the language spoken by the Aztec).

copal A hard resin—that is, a sticky, clear fluid—that flows from trees. Copal is made from tropical and subtropical trees and was burned as incense by the Aztec.

drought A long period of dry weather.

famine A lengthy period of food shortage that causes great hunger and death.

fertile Able to easily produce crops (when used about land or soil).

glyph A picture symbol in certain writing systems that could be used to stand for an idea, a sound, or a name.

jade A hard, tough, and highly colored stone. Jade comes in a wide range of colors, including dark green, white, yellow, gray, red, and black.

legend A folk story, often set in the past, which may be based in truth, but which may also contain fictional or fantastic elements. Legends are similar to **myths,** but myths often are about such sacred topics as gods or the creation of the world.

macuahuitl A club made of wood, with pieces of **obsidian** fixed to the edge.

maguey One of several kinds of agave plants that grow in the desert of what is now Mexico.

maze A network of paths designed to make it hard to find one's way through.

Mesoamerica The area that covers what is today Mexico and Central America.

myth See **legend.**

noble or **nobleman** or **-woman** A person of high standing in his or her culture.

obsidian A natural glass formed when hot lava flows onto the surface of Earth and cools quickly.

octli, also called pulque. An alcoholic drink made from the juice of the **maguey** plant.

patolli A board game played with beans marked with dots (similar to dice) and counters.

pochteca An Aztec merchant.

pyramid A large building or other structure with a square base and four smooth, triangular-shaped sides that come to a point at the top, or, in **Mesoamerica,** that were flat at the top.

ritual A solemn or important act or ceremony, often religious in nature.

scribe A specially trained person whose occupation is writing.

smallpox A deadly disease caused by a virus, *Variola major*. Smallpox spreads from person to person through the air.

social class A group of people who share a common status or position in society. Social classes represent differences in wealth, power, employment, family background, and other qualities.

tamale A food made of cornmeal paste and filled with beans or chilies, which is then wrapped in cornhusks and roasted or steamed.

telpochcalli A school for commoners.

terrace A small wall built by farmers to hold soil on a steep mountain slope.

tlatoani The ruler, or emperor, of the Aztec.

tortilla A thin, flat, round cake made of corn meal.

tribute Money or goods paid by one nation or group to another, in return for peace or protection

turquoise A mineral widely used as a gemstone; turquoise ranges in color from sky-blue to blue-green or yellow-green.

ullamaliztli An ancient ball game played on a court.

ADDITIONAL RESOURCES

Books

The Ancient Aztecs
by Liz Sonneborn (Franklin Watts, 2005)

The Aztec
by Andrew Santella (Children's Press, 2002)

The Aztec News
by Philip Steele (Candlewick Press, 1997)

The Aztecs: Rise and Fall of a Great Empire
by Roger Smalley (Red Brick Learning, 2004)

Hernando Cortes and the Fall of the Aztecs
by Rachel A. Koestler-Grack (Chelsea House,
2006)

History and Activities of the Aztecs
by Lisa Klobuchar (Heinemann Library, 2007)

How to Be an Aztec Warrior
by Fiona MacDonald (National Geographic, 2005)

National Geographic Investigates Ancient Aztec
by Tim Cooke (National Geographic, 2007)

The Secret World of the Aztecs
by Ferdinand Anton, translated by Paul Aston
(Prestel, 2002)

You Wouldn't Want to Be an Aztec Sacrifice!
by Fiona MacDonald (Franklin Watts, 2001)

Web Sites

http://home.freeuk.net/elloughton13/mexico.htm

http://www.azteccalendar.com/azteccalendar.html

http://www.elbalero.gob.mx/kids/history/html/conquista/aztecas.html

http://www.indians.org/welker/aztec.htm

http://www.kidspast.com/world-history/0281-aztecs.php

http://www.mexicolore.co.uk/index.php?one=azt&two=aaa

http://www.mnsu.edu/emuseum/cultural/mesoamerica/aztec.html

INDEX

Acamapichtli 8
Adobe 44
Agave plant 21
Ahuitzotl 10–11
Alabaster 23
Aqueducts 36
Archaeologists 5, 11, 37, 58
Armies 7–10, 12, 14, 16–17, 41, 55, 57
Art 40–41
Atlatls 17
Aztec empire (rise and fall of) 4, 6–12, 36, 52, 54–57

Bartering 19
Birds 15, 18–19, 32, 46, 50
Boats 53
Books 38–39
Bows and arrows 17, 48

Cacao beans 19, 47
Cactus 21
Calendars 34–35, 41
Calmecacs 33, 37, 49
Calpolli 14, 27
Canals 36, 49, 53
Caravans 18
Causeways 9, 36, 55–56
Childbirth 22–23, 48
Children 22, 31, 33, 43, 48–49
Chinampas 7, 20, 46
Chocolate 47, 59
Christianity 53, 57
Cities 5, 7–10, 19, 36–37, 57
Climate 4, 9, 20–21, 43
Cloth 19, 22, 24, 49, 52
Clothing 10, 13–15, 24, 44
Coatepec 39
Coatlicue 29
Codices 10, 13, 15, 18, 20–21, 26–27, 29, 31, 34, 38–39, 43, 45–46, 49, 51–53
Columbus, Christopher 54–55
Commoners 14–15, 18, 26, 30, 33, 39, 41, 45, 50
Copal 22, 30, 33, 44
Copper 19

Corn 21–23, 42, 46, 48
Cortés, Hernán 13, 19, 54, 56–57
Cotton 19, 21
Crafts 40–41
Craftsmen 14, 15, 19, 40–41, 42
Crime 24, 26–27, 53
Crops 4, 7, 14, 20–21, 35, 46, 51
Cuba 55

Day of the Dead 51, 59
Diaz del Castillo, Bernal 13, 24, 31, 57
Dogs 42
Drinks 47
Drought 8, 9, 21, 54

Eagle, snake, and cactus 7, 59
Eagle warriors 9, 16
Eagles 10, 16, 19
Education 13–17, 27, 33, 43, 48–49

Families 14, 22–23, 26, 42–43, 48–49
Famine 9, 12, 54
Farmers 14, 19, 20–21
Farming 6, 7, 14, 20–21, 35, 42–43
Feathers 10, 15–16, 19, 22, 41, 52
Festivals 35, 42, 47, 50–51, 59
Food 7, 21–22, 42–44, 46–47, 58-59

Games 50–51
Gardens 43, 44, 50
Glyphs 38–39
Gods and goddesses 12, 16, 18, 21–22, 28–34, 38, 47–48, 51
Gold 10, 17, 19, 23, 41, 47, 55
Government 13, 14, 49
Guatemala 5, 11, 55
Gulf Coast 5
Gulf of Mexico 10

Hairstyles 16–17
Headdresses 10, 15, 41
Helmets 9, 16
Herbs (medicinal) 19, 41
Horses 18
Houses 13–14, 30, 42–45
Housework 22, 42–43, 48

Huitzilopochtli 29, 37, 51
Human sacrifice 5, 11, 16, 24, 28, 30–31, 35, 51, 59
Hunting 50

Islands 7, 8, 20, 36
Itzcoatl 24–25

Jaguars 11, 29, 35, 41
Jewelry 12–13, 23, 27, 41, 45, 52, 59

Lakes 4, 7–9, 20, 36, 53
Language 38–39, 42, 58–59
Law 12, 26–27
Legends 6-7, 10
Livestock 21, 43, 46
Loincloths 14, 45, 53

Maguey plant 14, 21, 45, 47
Markets 14, 18–19, 22, 24, 35–36, 46, 52–53, 58
Marriage 22, 26, 42
Maya 5, 34
Merchants 14–15, 18–19, 47, 52
Mesoamerica 4, 6, 10, 34, 38, 51–52, 54
Mexica 6
Mexico 4–6, 10, 49, 55, 58
Mexico City 4, 8, 11, 14, 16, 37, 40, 57–58
Midwives 23, 48
Mirrors 41
Mixtec 9, 12, 34
Money 19
Montezuma I 8-10, 26–27
Montezuma II 10–11, 46, 55–57
Motherhood 22
Mountains 4, 20, 37
Music 50
Myths 4, 28, 29

Nahuatl 38–39, 42, 58–59
Nobles 12–16, 18–19, 23, 26–27, 30–31, 33, 39, 40–41, 43, 45–47, 49–50

Obsidian 17, 31, 41, 48, 53
Olmec 5
Oral history 6

Pacific Coast 9–10
Palaces 5, 12, 27, 36, 40, 44
Porters 18, 53
Priests 13, 15, 30–33, 35, 37, 39, 41, 45, 48–49
Prisoners 5, 11, 13, 15–17, 24, 26
Punishments 24, 26–27, 47–49, 53
Pyramids 4–5, 30–31, 36–37, 40, 58

Quetzal birds 18, 41

Rainfall 20–21, 51
Raw materials 18, 52
Religion 4–5, 12, 16, 22, 26, 28–33, 35, 37, 39, 47, 50, 53, 57
Rivers 20
Rulers 8–13, 24– 27, 44

Sandals 14, 27, 45
Schools *see* Education
Scribes 39
Sculpture 14, 33, 40–41
Servants 15
Shields 10, 48
Ships 12
Shrines (household) 22, 30, 41, 44
Silver 19, 23, 41
Slaves 24–25, 37, 53
Smallpox 57
Snake Woman 12
Snakes 7, 37, 41

Social class system 15, 18, 24, 26
Soldiers 8–9, 12–13, 15–18, 57
Spanish (people) 4, 8, 10, 12–13, 19, 49, 53–57
Sport 50–51
Swamps 7, 20, 36–37
Sun (Aztec beliefs about) 29, 31
Sun Stone 40–41, 58

Tamales 46
Tarascan 10–11
Taxes 10, 14
Telpochcalli 49
Temples 5, 8, 9, 11, 14, 16, 22, 30–33, 37, 40, 43
Templo Mayor 8, 11, 16, 31–33, 36–37, 40, 56, 58
Tenochtitlan 5, 7–11, 32, 36–37, 41, 52, 54–57, 59
Teotihuacan 4
Tepanec 8–9
Terraces 20
Terra cotta 16, 32
Teteoinnan 29
Texcoco City 9, 27
Texcoco, Lake 5, 7–8, 55
Tezcatlipoca 29, 41
Tlacopan 9
Tlaloc 28–29, 33, 37
Tlatelolco 8, 10, 19, 24, 36, 50, 52

Tlatoani 8–14, 18, 24, 26–27, 30, 40–41, 44, 47, 54, 57
Tlaxcala 54, 57
Toci 29
Toltec 5
Tonatiuh 23, 29, 40–41
Tools 20, 53
Tortillas 22, 46, 59
Trade 18–19, 52–53
Transportation 18, 52–53
Tribute 10, 24, 52, 54
Triple Alliance 8–9
Turquoise 23, 30, 41

United States 18, 58

Valley of Mexico 4, 6, 8–9, 19, 20, 22, 54
Veracruz 12
Volcanoes 4, 17

Wars 9–10, 12, 16–18, 22, 57
Weapons 17
Weaving 22, 45
Weddings 22
Wheels 53
Women 13, 22–23, 30, 42, 44–45, 48–49
Writing 38–39

Zorita, Anthony de 49

Acknowledgments

The Art Archive: 7 (Museo Ciudad, Mexico), 10 (Bodleian Library, Oxford), 13, 15 (Antiochiw Collection, Mexico/ Mireille Vautier), 16 (Museo del Templo Mayor, Mexico), 17 (Museo Etnografico Pigorini, Rome), 22 (Archaeological Museum, Teotihuacan, Mexico), 25, 26 (Mireille Vautier), 29 (National Archives, Mexico/ Mireille Vautier), 31, 33, 43 (Templo Mayor Library, Mexico), 44, 45, 46 (Templo Mayor Library, Mexico), 49 (Bodleian Libary, Oxford), 51 (Bibliothêque de l'Assemblée Nationale, Paris), 52 (Templo Mayor Library, Mexico), 54 (Biblioteca Nacional, Madrid), 55 (Museo Ciudad, Mexico); **Bridgeman Art Library**: 12 (Baluarete de Santiago, Veracruz, Mexico/ Michael Zabe/ AZA), 14 (Museo Nacional de Antropologia, Mexico/ Bildarchiv Steffens), 20 (Biblioteca Medicea-Laurenziana, Florence), 27 (Biblioteca Medicea-Laurenziana, Florence), 40 (Museo Nacional de Arqueologia, Mexico City © AISA), 53 (Biblioteca Medicea-Laurenziana, Florence), 56 (Archives Charmet), 57 (Glasgow University Library; **Corbis**: 5 (Danny Lehman), 37 (Nik Wheeler), 58 (Patrick Frilet/Hemis), 59 (Danny Lehman); www.mexicolore.co.uk: 42; **Topfoto**: 11 (Richard Pitcairn-Knowles); **Werner Forman Archive**: 1 (Museo Etnografico Pigorini, Rome), 4, 8, 9, 18, 21, 23, 24 (Merrin Collection), 28 (Philip Goldman), 30 (Museo Etnografico Pigorini, Rome), 32 (Portland Art Museum, Oregon), 34 (Biblioteca Universitaria, Bologna), 35 (Museo Nacional de Arqueologia, Mexico City), 38 (Liverpool Museum, Liverpool), 39 (Liverpool Museum, Liverpool), 41 (British Museum, London), 47 (Museo Nacional de Arqueologia, Mexico City), 48 (Museum fur Volkerkunde, Basel), 50 (British Museum, London); **World Book**: 36.

Cover image: **Alamy Images** (John Mitchell)
Back cover image: **Shutterstock** (Joop Snijder, Jr.)